HOW TO STAY OUT OF JAIL

Advice for BIPOC and The Poor

Donald H. Matthews, PhD.

Faith DonnaMarada Matthews, Illustrator

PARE University Place, WA September 1, 2021

TABLE OF CONTENTS

ACKNOWLEDGEMENTS

We are living in troubled times. In times like these it is important to acknowledge all the support that we receive from family, friends and from the many nameless acquaintances that make the difference in our lives. As regards to this book, I recognize the men and women who have faced jailing and prison incarceration under circumstances that do not give credit to our understanding of what it means to be an ideal person of any valued tradition. There has been much written about the history of incarceration, its excesses, and injustices. This book does not attempt to compete with those which seek to present a more academic understanding of how we got to this point in our history except to make broad references to this situation in the fourth part which considers social theory and jailing.

Instead, it is meant to be more personal in its method and its telling of the story of the many who have been incarcerated. I experienced the shame and fear associated with being stopped by police officers over twenty times just for being Black. One of my proudest moments was when one of the students at Naropa University, Quddus Maus, informed me that the political prisoner, Mumia Abu-Jamal, referenced one of my books in his writing. My experience of finally settling the issue that led to my own jailing eleven years after my arrest was the immediate stimulus for the writing of this small book.

The world of jail and prison has acted as an unseen, but ever present factor that myself and other Black men live with on a daily basis. It is a possibility that looms with every public or private action that has even the remotest possibility of being the cause for the intervention of the police. I write this book with the belief that prevention is more important than experiencing jail. My hope is that this text will provide a theology and philosophy for the common person, especially those who are from marginalized communities, which will help them avoid jailing and incarceration.

As always, I had the support of my daughter, Faith Matthews, who illustrated the cover for this book. Her artwork offers a symbolic representation of my subject matter that I can then refine in the final editing of my writings. My life-partner, Linda M. Knowlton, provided the love, space and resources necessary for me to write this book and deal with the criminal justice system amidst a pandemic. I thank my friends; Facebook and in person. When I wanted to reject a plea deal and risk serving time, those closest to me thought it better that I skip my self-martyrdom and write about my experiences instead. A special thanks goes to Sr. Thea Joy Browne SSG PhD., for her comments on New Testament interpretation.

Most importantly, this book is dedicated to the recent and past hundreds of thousands who have been the victims of a justice system that was never designed to protect them. A new generation of scholars, attorneys and Black Lives Matter activists are trying to rewrite that script.

I never got the chance to meet my maternal Great Uncle Bill, who spent hard time in the notorious Parchment Prison in Mississippi. May you Rest in Peace after having experienced some of the worst conditions of life that America had to offer. Live eternally with your compassionate Maker.

Donald H. Matthews, PhD., The Homeless Professor

September 2021, University Place, WA 98467

donhmatt@yahoo.com

THE SITUATION*

BLACK MEN HAVE THE HIGHEST MORTALITY RATE OF ANY RACIAL GROUP.

BLACK MEN WITH A BACHELOR'S DEGREE ARE PAID 30% LESS THAN WHITE MEN WITH A BACHELOR'S DEGREE.

ONLY 50% OF BLACK MALES GRADUATE FROM HIGH SCHOOL.

OVER ONE MILLION OUT OF 19 MILLION BLACK MEN ARE INCARCERATED.

BLACK MALES EXPERIENCE HOMELESSNESS MORE THAN ANY RACIAL GROUP.

BLACK MALE UNEMPLOYMENT IS DOUBLE THE RATE AT EVERY EDUCATIONAL LEVEL.

BLACK MALES ARE THREE TIMES MORE IN NEED OF SUBSTANCE ABUSE

TREATMENT

AND THE BEAT GOES ON

THERE WAS A BLACK BOY*

There was a Black boy who was killed because he looked at a
White woman.
There was a Black boy who had his first sexual experience when
he was six years old.
There was a Black boy whose mother disciplined him
with an iron skillet.
There was a Black boy who committed suicide
because he was queer.
There was a Black boy who was killed by police because he
"fit the description."
There was a Black boy who was almost kidnapped when he
was eight years old.
There was a Black boy who was murdered because he was
slinging dope.
There was a Black boy who lost his childhood because he was
sexualized.
There was a Black boy who was constantly beaten by
gangbangers in his hood.
There was a Black boy who was profiled by police because he
was in a White area.
There was a Black boy who did time even though he didn't do
the crime.

There was a Black boy who was killed by White vigilantes for walking down the street.
There was a Black boy who left his home because there was not enough room.
There was a Black boy who was attacked by White gangbangers on the White side of the street.
There was a Black boy who was sodomized by his older sister.
There was a Black boy who was homeless because his parents were out of work. There was a Black boy who was assaulted by his White gym teacher
There was a Black boy who turned to crime because he could not read.
There was a Black boy who was lynched because he wanted to be free.
There was a Black boy who couldn't concentrate because he was hungry.
There was a Black boy who was shy because he only had one pair of pants.
There was a Black boy who was molested by his babysitter.
There was a Black boy who committed suicide because his foster life was too painful There was a Black boy who turned to crime because his father was in jail.
There was a Black boy who was kicked by his White coach.

There was a Black boy who became depressed because his peers called him a fag.

There was a Black boy who was too "girlish", so he ruined his life by being "manly."

There was a Black boy whose mother neglected him.

There was a Black boy who saw his father beat his mother.

There was a Black boy who ran his tricycle off a landing and died.

There was a Black boy who drowned while his White friends watched.

There was a Black boy who tried to be a daddy when he was still a son.

There was a Black boy who came to school dirty because his mama was in jail.

There were BLACK boys whose fathers were nowhere to be seen or heard.

I wonder why.

"Destroying Black Males," DHM

INTRODUCTION

There is a time for everything, and a season for every activity under the heavens: a time to be born, and a time to die; a time to plant, and a time to pluck up that which is planted; a time to kill, and a time to heal; a time to break down, and a time to build up; a time to weep, and a time to laugh; a time to mourn, and a time to dance...a time to be silent and a time to speak. A time to love and a time to hate, a time for war and a time for peace,

Ecclesiastes 3rd Chapter

I have written this book in Wisdom traditional style that is found in Ancient Black Writings and in the Hebrew Bible. It is a kind of advice book that is meant to give practical advice to persons of color and other people in our society who face social oppression and therefore are more likely to find themselves in trouble with the law and in jail. It is a highly biographical book that features much of my own personal experience as a Black man and as a minister and professor who has mentored many persons who have found themselves in trouble with the criminal justice system, myself included. It is not a so-called "objective" look at the criminal justice system. How in the world can you have an objective opinion about a topic in which the subject's life is so dependent? My hope is that it is written in a plain and clear style that will be easily read and understood by everyday people.

The advice is inspired by my understanding of this ancient Wisdom tradition that is most accessible in the world's bestselling book: The Holy Bible. The Wisdom literature in the Old Testament or Hebrew Bible and the sayings of Jesus and his followers in the Christian New Testament, if read correctly, gives us a perspective that was used by the ancients to keep the regular person from undue harm from oppressive government systems. I debated whether I would include chapter and verse where these messages are found but I believe that this would place too much burden on the narrative.

If one wishes to understand the context and content of these Biblical perspectives, I suggest that one should read the Bible as one would read literature. I have gained the most insights and understanding by simply becoming familiar with the texts. The bible is full of characters who had to deal with authorities that represented the power of the national governments for which they were citizens or immigrants. The biblical stories tell of strategies of survival in hostile social environments whether the possible violence comes from within their home nation or foreign powers.

The arbitrary and unfair use of power by these systems often resulted in jail, execution, torture, and exile for those who sought to simply live in peace without being negatively affected by police brutality. Those who directly opposed the unjust systems are called "Prophets," not just because they predicted future events but because they identified and spoke against unjust social practices. The goal of the prophets was to bring justice to their world in the face of evil. The biblical prophets were all about freedom and justice for the everyday person who had to struggle to make a living for themselves and their families.

Too often the Christian Scriptures found in the New Testament are not interpreted in a way that brings out their use as a strategy for the early Christians in their efforts to" "to stay out of jail." Even those who would interpret Hebrew scriptures as being more concerned with so called "spiritual" matters, rather than the creation of a just society, have been duped by powerful religious institutions who are more interested in maintaining their power than in the safety of the common person. How else could the story of Noah's ark become a tale which is interpreted as a story that warns against disobedience of God's direction, rather than a story about a just God who condemns the world because humans are violent against one another. It is not a story of belief in God. It is a story about humankind's decision to violate the will of God who wishes persons to live in peace and harmony. The Christian preoccupation with sin often forgets that the specific sin that triggers the Great Flood was the sin of violence in society. I will look at the words and actions of Jesus as he taught his followers how to stay out of jail.

PART ONE

TEN THINGS TO KNOW WHEN DEALING WITH THE CRIMINAL JUSTICE SYSTEM

1- Truth and evidence.

Truth is relative to the situation in which one finds oneself. It is ironic that the American Pragmatic School of Philosophy led by American philosophers like John Dewey and Josiah Royce demonstrated that truth is only possible when there is an important issue at stake. Instead of wondering about some abstract concept of truth, they like Jesus, understood that the truth is only understood by those who are affected by it.

The truth is never as simple as one thinks. When Jesus was placed on trial before Pontius Pilate, the representative of European Imperial power of his day, he refused to answer when Pilate asked him; "What is Truth?" Jesus understood that his truth would never be understood by a person whose livelihood and mission was to conquer and oppress the People of Color and the Poor.

This is the reason why police search for evidence instead of simply accepting the testimony of persons as they tell their version of the truth. Instead , it is necessary to determine some more objective way of determining the truth of a particular situation. The truth may be different for different people in different social situations. In terms of the criminal justice system, never believe that "truth" is on your side. This is especially true in our criminal justice system which is adversarial by design. Your truth may not be the truth of witnesses, a jury, judge, or district attorney who may be representative of the powerful and wealthy members of a community that do not share your ethnicity or values.

2- Justice System is often an "Unjust System."

The famous poem written about the justice system applies here.:

Justice:

"That justice is a blind goddess Is something to which we Blacks are wise:

Her bandage hides two festering sores, that once perhaps were eyes

Langston Hughes' poem is a play on the idea that "justice is blind," meaning that all persons should be judged without bias due to any trait they may have. Neither race, religion, gender, or any other factor should interfere with the handing out of a just verdict. The history of America has found that this kind of justice has been sorely lacking throughout its history. Juries are chosen by prosecuting and defense attorneys who know that social minorities are much more likely to be convicted by persons not of their racial and socioeconomic status.

3- What is right may not be legal. What is legal may not be right.

What may seem to be an obvious case of right or wrong may not be true when it comes to the legal process. This is one reason for the statement: "Only a fool has himself for a client." The regular citizen has little idea of how the legal process works or how to proceed in complicated legal proceedings. The presiding judge may help the unrepresented client, but they will always be behind in knowledge and expertise in how to conduct a case. Here, once again, the popular media has done the public no favor by picturing heroic stories where prison inmates have become “jailhouse” lawyers who are able to expertly conduct their cases. The actual instances of this happening are so few and far between that they have no real-world reality.

The justice system is about the right legal process, not the right moral position. Do not believe what you see on the crime dramas on TV and the movies. If you do not have social status or and/or money, you are likely to be charged and convicted of a crime.

4- District Attorney

The District Attorney (DA) and the District Attorney’s Office are the most important person and structure in the Criminal Justice system. They are the ones who determine if, when, and what you will face as far as criminal charges are concerned. The police and District Attorney (including the assistant DAs who conduct the trials) work closely together. The DAs seldom contradict the police officers’ decision to charge a person with a crime unless the person has a high social status due to race, money, position, or other factors.

5- Judge

The judge rarely contradicts the police or the District Attorney. Once again, the picture you get from watching popular television series, like Law and Order, where there is a constant battle between the police, the judges and the district attorney rarely happens. These three entities; the judges, the district attorneys and the police are not on your side. It is an adversarial system, and you are the adversary. They rub and protect each other's backs to maintain their power and order in society.

6- The Public Defender

The Public Defender that is assigned to you, if you do not have the money to hire your own lawyer, is hired and works for and with the District Attorney's Office. Their job is to expedite cases by convincing you to accept a plea deal that will usually result in a conviction, but with less jail time or fines. The Public Defenders and District Attorneys do not want to spend their time, effort, and the taxpayer's money in conducting trials. Instead, they want to pad their statistics of convicted criminals to demonstrate that they are worthy of being elected, reelected, or are prepared to take on higher public responsibilities.

YOUR ADVOCATES

7-Private Attorneys

Even if you have an attorney, your attorney wants to stay on the good side of the District Attorneys and their Assistant District attorneys who will prosecute your case. Depending on the size of the municipality and age and experience of your attorney, he or she may be on a friendly first name basis with the prosecuting attorneys and judges. It is all about association and keeping a good relationship with the DA and Judges. This can affect your case for good or bad. The outcome of your case is often dependent on the effectiveness of your attorney. There are some defense attorneys who truly have your interest in heart and will do their best to defend you, while at the same time understanding the bias and defects in the Criminal Justice system.

8-Cash is King.

Your class and caste status will play a huge role in determining whether you are going to be charged, sentenced, and going to jail. The system in a capitalist, materialist society looks more favorably on those with wealth and power. Democratic principles are secondary to issues of power and privilege. If you are White or wealthy, you will be much less likely to go to jail. If you are charged, the success of your defense will be heavily based on how much money you can devote for your defense. This is also true of the fines and bail process. If you are not able to make bail or pay fines, it is not unusual that you will be placed in jail until your trial. This may take several months and sometimes years depending on the nature of the case.

The more money you have, can beg, or borrow will be crucial to your staying out of jail, although it must be used wisely. Jesus said that the love of money was the root of all evil. But without money, it is more likely that the evil that can only be handed out by the criminal justice system is likely to be your faith. It is ironic that Americans are proud of having started a revolution because they deemed the taxes of England to be unjust.

9- Community Pressure is Divine.

What history has taught us is that government and social agencies will respond if the community pressure is great.

The Civil Rights Movement and The Black Urban Rebellions resulted in numerous positive changes for the oppressed Black community. Other socially marginalized people like: Women, Gay and Queer community, Migrant workers, Muslim immigrants, etc. followed suit and won victories for their constituencies.

This is true for personally based crimes as well. It will always work in your favor if you can bring your need to others when involved with the criminal justice system. Mothers Against Drunk Driving (MADD) is a perfect example. This is a matter of self-protection against, bias, undue force, and illegal treatment. Persons who can show that there are persons in their community that care about them are much more likely to be treated more leniently by the criminal justice system. Community support can translate into support or non-support for the future elections of judges and district attorneys. The police are also much more likely to treat those under their jurisdiction with respect and care if they know that they will be held accountable by their community.

10-Social Media is a powerful tool

It is important to put your case out to the public. The system is already stacked against you and is designed to limit your ability to a fair hearing with your peers as judge. If you are a minority or poor, you are less likely to get a fair trial, your peers are not likely to be represented on any jury panel. Juries, by their very nature and selection, tend to be composed of persons who have not had an unpleasant or unjust relationship with the police and the criminal justice system. In fact, the police are meant to protect their White and middle-class persons from people like you.

If you have never seen the film "12 Angry Men," you should. In this film Henry Fonda is cast as the lone juror who believes that it is important to carefully consider the evidence. The other jurors, eleven White men, exhibit their prejudice against persons of color and the poor by rushing to judgement without considering the life changing implications of their decision on the young plaintiff. However, Henry Fonda's character eventually, with great care and perseverance, convince the other jury members to look beyond their stated prejudices and they set the ethnic minority youth free.

Unfortunately, this kind of advocacy rarely occurs in our court system. As was seen in the Rodney King case, the police officers were exonerated by a White jury who did not consider what their eyes had seen, the brutal beating of a defenseless Black man by multiple police officers. Johnnie Cochran, the famed defense attorney who successfully defended O.J. Simpson, understood how important the jury makeup is for either acquitting or convicting the defendants. Despite claims otherwise, the jury is more likely to have obvious or unconscious biases that may interfere with their ability to make reasonable judgements and Mr. Cochran understood the feelings of powerlessness and anger that most Black citizens had against the criminal justice system.

Currently social media was the all-important factor as to the conviction of Officer Chauvin, who brutally murdered George Floyd. The video tape of the savage treatment of Floyd by Chauvin could not be denied. However, even with that kind of evidence, as was seen in the cases of the murders of Eric Garner and Michael Grant, police officers are not likely to be charged and convicted by a White populace that fears Blacks and people of color. As long as America remains separate by race and color, it is important to rely on social media and other forms of protest to insure justice.

Summary

The "Show Trial of Officer Chauvin," in the George Floyd murder case illustrates many of the previous statements. When the State Attorney General got involved, millions of dollars were used to prosecute Chauvin. This is not likely to happen to the average BIPOC or poor person. It was nice to see justice done for Brother Floyd, but it had little spillover effect on the conduct of police officers as they continued to assault men, women, boys, and girls of color after the trial was over. In the meantime, I am offering some personal advice that may help you keep out of jail and free of the clutches of the "United States Injustice System."

PART TWO

TESTIMONIES

This chapter will present several real-life scenarios that are examples of how Black persons, BIPOC and poor people are in constant danger of going to jail. My discussion of these instances will make obvious some of the principles I discussed in the previous chapters. I will begin with some of my experiences from childhood to the present.

WALKING WHILE BLACK—14 years old

The first time I was called a nigger was when I was fourteen years old. It was a White preschooler who had been taught by his parents that the teens he saw in his neighborhood were not Black, Negro, African American or Colored. They were referred to as Niggers.

He was playing in his fenced-in yard as my buddies, and I were walking to school after getting off the 63rd Street bus on the way to Lindblom Technical High School. Lindblom was a school for those of us who had excellent test scores and grades in grammar school. We had all taken the entrance test and done well enough to be invited to attend the school.

The high school was in a formerly White neighborhood that was going through transition from Caucasian to predominantly Black. White families were in full flight as more and more Black families were leaving the inner-city ghettos and buying homes in their White neighborhood. When my older brother Alvin attended Lindblom two years earlier, it was approximately 50% White. It was less than 10% White by the time I attended the school. What we now call "gentrification" in which Blacks were removed from their neighborhoods due to its proximity to the downtown areas, real estate agents and banks were convincing Whites to sell their homes to the incoming Blacks. They made a profit from the Whites who gave in to their scare tactics; and from Blacks who wanted a better housing situation for themselves and their families.

As my Black schoolmates and I walked past the child, he said: "HI Niggers!" He was not much older than four years old. My schoolmates told me that his parents put him up to this, knowing we would not attack a child. In fact, we could see his mother standing in the doorway watching her child as he insulted us. And so, we replied "Hi little nigger. Have a nice day" and we kept on stepping. One afternoon we were walking past the same house on the way to the bus stop. Only this time there was a patrol car in front of the house. The Officer left his car to tell us that the people in the house reported an incident of "harassment of their son" against her son.

The police officer told some of us to get in the squad car and after we got in the car, he began asking us for our personal information. What was our names and addresses, he asked? I just sat there not saying a word. After a few minutes, the policeman let us go with a warning. My buddies who were not placed in the car, asked us what happened. My friends expressed admiration and wonder when they stated that "Matt didn't say a word. He's a bad dude." I was just fourteen at the time and was just coming to an understanding of how racism had affected Black folks in the US of A. What my friends did not know, and what I did not tell them, was that I was a stutterer; especially when I was nervous. I did not say anything to the officer for fear that I would stutter, and that the officer would think I was afraid of him if I had stammered in his presence. It had not occurred to me that he could have arrested me for obstruction of justice or some other made-up charge.

That neighborhood felt the full wrath of our pent-up anger at the way we were treated as we went to school in their neighborhood and in America the day after Martin Luther King, Jr was killed. Unwisely, the School Board kept the schools open after King's assassination. When we arrived at school that day, the entire student body was told to report to the assembly hall where we were to be allowed to grieve King's assassination. The few Black teachers tried to get us to remain cool and talked about King's philosophy of non-violence. Since we had all witnessed the hostility that King received when he had come to Chicago to protest racial discrimination, we were not having it. Instead, the teachers were booed off the stage, the fire alarms were pulled, and a thousand students rushed out into the surrounding neighborhood. The angry students marched through the all-White neighborhood and caused quite a bit of havoc as pay back for the many insults we had received. I and most of my friends were so afraid that we had little interest in payback. We wanted to get home before the National Guard was called up and the police force reacted with undue force. Instead, we went straight to the bus stop as the surrounding neighborhoods were engulfed by the Black rage of the angry youth.

MENTALLY ILL WHILE BLACK

Marley Baby

Marley Baby was my first roommate at Northwestern University. We had gone to the same elementary and high schools and decided that we wanted to be roommates that first year of college. We lived about four city blocks from each other in the deepest hood on the Southside of Chicago. He lived in the Projects, a high-rise urban ghetto, and I lived in a house closer to our elementary school.

Marley was an extremely thin boy who used his gift of gab and effervescent personality to keep him safe from the local gangs in his housing unit. When we discussed our college plans, he pledged that he would never do drugs because of the damage he had seen them do to his own friends and family in the community. The Black ghettos were flooded with drugs in the late sixties to hook as many frustrated young Blacks as possible into the use, abuse and selling of illicit drugs.

After my father drove us to the dorm at Northwestern, we settled in. As I mentioned; Marley was extremely gifted in speech and in making friends. He was the prime organizer, college promoter and M.C. when The Funkadelic Parliament came to perform at our campus. He was resplendent that night in the psychedelic clothing of the seventies. With Marley's urging and example, we left our seats to get on the stage and shake our booties to the funky, funky music.

Later in our first year Marley was befriended by an older brother who had seen duty in the Navy in Vietnam. This brother was an avid user of pot and alcohol, and it did not take long before Marley forgot his pledge of sobriety. Marley and his friend would spend many nights getting high in our small dorm room. I was too tired from football practice and staying up late in the library where I worked and studied to let it affect my sleep, although a contact high was a constant possibility.

I have a friend, Doug W, who believed that much of the pot in those days was also laced with various chemicals which could cause neurological damage. He may be right. Marley went from being a popular man on the campus, even as a freshman, to being dysfunctional in his behavior. He became more and more withdrawn and spent more time getting high than paying attention to his studies. He left school after his first year and I did not see him until years later when I was in graduate school, working late at night at the Reference Desk in the library.

As he sat talking to me behind the Reference Desk counter, he climbed on the counter itself and began to contort himself into different positions on the counter. I asked what the deal was, and he said he was doing yoga. When I asked why; he said that the yoga made him more limber from when the men in prison demanded sex. It turned out that he had spent some time in jail in Minnesota for passing bad checks. To survive without extreme bodily harm, he had to comply with their wishes. He said it so matter of factly that his response took me off guard. His affect was different. He was there, but not there at the same time. Something in him had obviously snapped. He did not have the money to defend himself against the charges and took the plea deal.

He was also carrying my High School yearbook, which he had "borrowed" from me some four years earlier; the last time we saw each other. I guess it was a keep's sake that reminded him of his former achievements and glory. When I left the Reference Desk to shelve some books and do some other work; he had vanished with my yearbook in hand. Several years later I saw him walking the streets of the Southside of Chicago. He told me his mother had thrown him out of her apartment and he was homeless. I arranged for him to stay in an empty bedroom in our home on the Southside but after a week he was asked to leave because of his disruptive behavior.

The last time I saw him was some ten years later when I went to graduate school in Chicago. He now lived in a group home for the chronically mentally ill. He spent his days waking the streets until it was time for him to check into his group home. He would hold a normal conversation and then abruptly break into an undecipherable line of speech. That was the last time I saw Marley Baby. I hope that wherever he is, he is well. He was a brilliant young Black man who had much to give to our society. This story demonstrates what happens to folks who do not have access to adequate mental health and legal resources. It is obvious to me now that he was struggling with his addiction even as he swore never to engage in drugs. Jail has become the largest haven for the Black mentally ill male. Without adequate social nets and legal assistance that kind of fall from grace is inevitable. Jail is an inevitable destination when a person does not have the financial and social supports necessary to survive the mean streets of our society.

When I worked with Lu W., as a Co-Director of a Spiritual Support Group with parents of mentally ill children. The ways in which even these White women, were forced to become advocates with the criminal justice system indicated an even more severe problem for families of Color. The group members were able to share various strategies and resources for dealing with the police, mental health professionals and the court system. It became obvious to me that the children of Black persons were treated with less care than the children of White parents. But, having the assistance of a White, dedicated social justice advocate like Lu meant a great deal in gaining access to resources for the Black boys and men who were in conflict with the system.

At one point I was asked to speak at a regional meeting of The Interfaith Network on Mental Illness which was held at the University of Colorado Law School in Boulder, CO. I was a Speaker and Panelist with other mental health professionals who shared their experiences concerning the difficulty that persons with mental health issues had in both receiving adequate treatment and avoiding incarceration due to mental illness. The continued shooting of mentally ill persons by police officers who have little training in this area speaks to the great need for our society to develop policies and procedures that keep safe the afflicted person and those who may be endangered by their erratic behavior.

The best course would be to develop community mental health resources that would work outside of, or in conjunction with police forces when absolutely necessary. I remember back in the day that a family member could call mental health workers to take their loved ones, often against their will, to facilities where they could receive adequate treatment.

STANDING WHILE BLACK

The Black community developed the term: "DWB" (Driving While Black) to label the frequent stops by police officers who pulled over Black persons, especially males, as a form of intimidation and harassment. I have been stopped over 20 times while DWB. Black males also experience "SWB," (Standing While Black) "WWB," (Walking While Black) "SIWB" (Sitting While Black) and other forms of police incursion in their lives. This includes "HWB" (Housing While Black: Breanna Taylor, Fred Hampton) as police officers have been known to violate the sanctity of the homes of Black persons for purposes of "crime fighting," or as a tool for assassination (The Murder of Fred Hampton; the MOVE Bombing in Philly).

I was Standing While Black on an L (Elevated) Platform on the Northside of Chicago waiting for the public train in the 80'S with a woman friend who was White. It was a cold Chicago night and so we huddled together as a windbreak from the effects of "The Hawk." This was unusual for us since she was born and raised in Japan where public shows of affection are discouraged. And even though I seldom engaged in public displays of affection, I was glad to try and keep warm on a frigid Chicago night. The cold, cold, cold winter trumped social convention, so we stood as close together as possible to share some warmth.

After a couple of minutes one of "Chicago's finest" walked past us. I nodded in greeting; but he kept on walking without saying a word. Shortly thereafter we were surrounded by several White police officers. I was told to "assume the position" meaning that I was to face the wall with my hands on the wall and my feet spread. My friend, who was new to the ways of how Black men are treated in America, began to protest. I asked her to be cool lest she bring on the ire of the police officers which could have put me in danger of restraint or arrest.

Soon the police officer's Sergeant arrived on the scene and asked if I had been searched. The initial officer said no, and he began his search. As I was searched, the policeman found that I had my pipe in my coat pocket, but not a pot or crack pipe. It was a finely made English smoking pipe, not a crack pipe or a weapon as he expected. His countenance began to change as he began to realize that he had a made a mistake in treating me like a criminal. My friend was then encouraged to speak, and she asked what the problem was. The Sergeant responded that a woman who lived in the adjacent building noticed us and called in with a report of a White woman being held hostage at gunpoint by a Black man on the L platform.

The other White persons on the platform overheard the discussion. Without being asked, they got involved in the situation. They told the policemen that: "He probably threw his gun on the train tracks," and they pointed to where I must have tossed my nonexistent weapon. The policemen looked and saw that there was no gun thrown on the train tracks. As a matter of fact, I have never owned or shot a gun. The Sergeant apologized and said that since they had received the complaint that they had to check into it.

After the policemen left, I just stared in disbelief, anger, and amazement at the other passengers. Because I was a Black man in the company of a White woman, they had created a visual image of me having a weapon and throwing it away. The same was true of the woman who had made the report. It made me even more aware of the fear that White people have developed of Black males regardless of what common sense and even their physical senses tell them. I was placed in danger of being shot, arrested, and placed in jail because some nameless White female and a handful of my fellow White citizens assumed that I had kidnapped a White woman by use of a gun that did not exist.

Little Al

It was during the night of a hot summer day in 1986 in Oakland, California when I was visited by a spirit while I slept. It was during the early morning hours just before the breaking of the dawn when the dream world of sleep comes into an awareness of the unseen world of the Spirit. It was still dark; but it was such a powerful visitation that I was jarred awake. I had taken a course in Dream Analysis and so I knew that I should wake up and write down the dream while it was still in one's conscious awareness. So, I made a mental note, wrote down some of what I had been given and went back to sleep. What I had written was a eulogy. I did not know who it was for or why I had written it.

While I was still in bed and just coming out of my final sleep, I received a call from a relative. She told me that my nephew Al was dead and that she wanted me to come home and to officiate at his funeral service. I was in the midst of a PhD. Program at The Divinity School of the University of Chicago in the Psychology and Sociology of Religion. The mystery of the late-night visitation was now solved. It was for Al. It was his funeral sermon that I had sketched. The visitation I had experienced was AL's way of saying goodbye and a reminder to be remembered; which is why I am writing this section of this text. This kind of visitation is not unusual in my family or in other members of the Black and other spiritual communities who understand that there is more to life than what we see in this world.

During our conversation she told me that Al had been missing for several days. He recently attended summer school to graduate from Middle School and was excited to begin his High School journey. He had some difficulty in eighth grade but had turned the corner and was beginning to enjoy academic success. He was a bright and sensitive kid, who like many Black children, especially boys, just needed more encouragement and insight which was provided by his mother and a Black Male Pastoral Counselor.

To celebrate his impending graduation ceremony, he had gone to a Lake Michigan beach with some of his friends; all were White teens that he had befriended at school. However, he did not return home. When his friends were asked what happened to him and where he was, they all claimed that they did not know. This set off a flurry of prayers and searching but there was no luck in finding him. Hospitals were called, the police were called, but after a few days there was still no news of his whereabouts. Finally, his mother in a last act of desperation fell on her knees and in an act of supplication, she called on the Lord of Heaven and those Ancestors who had already gone to the Other Side. She told them that if she had ever done anything in her lifetime that was worthy of God's favor, then please let her know what had happened to her youngest child.

The next day she received a call from the police. They had retrieved Al's floating body from Lake Michigan several days before but due to the bloating of the body they assumed that he was a Black male in his thirties. And since it is not unusual that Black boys are often thought to be older than they are, it took the police longer to finally put two and two together and realize that he was in fact Al, the young teenager, for whom his family had been searching for.

Perhaps if he had gone swimming on the Southside of Chicago closer to home where most Black teens regularly went to swim, the authorities would not assumed have he was an older Black male. But he and his White friends had gone to the predominantly White Northside; and so, when his body was found he was treated like just another deceased Black male that had met his untimely end.

I flew back to Chicago and prepared, with the support of family and friends, to conduct the funeral service. It was the first, but it would not be the last, funeral I led for a family member, and one of many I would attend for dead Black youth. The funeral service was held on an oppressively hot and humid night for which the Midwest is infamous. The funeral home was packed with persons of all ages and races. Most of the young people had never been to a funeral before and so I began with words of comfort for them and thanked them for their presence

We never discovered what really happened to Al that summer day in Chicago. We could only speculate as whether his death was an accident, due to kids being kids; or if there was some foul play. The police did not do a thorough investigation. None of his fellow teens were interrogated or charged. Like so many Black families we did not know the exact circumstances of his death. Like those other families, we believe that what was done in secret will one day be revealed. It is a biblical hope, a karmic hope, that there is justice in the next world if not in this one.

The fact that his friends did not inform his sister or mother that he had drowned suggests that some foul play or negligence was involved. At one point one of their Youth

Advisors, a White female ministry student, told me that these youth wondered if they could talk to me about it confidentially. I had managed to control my anger over his untimely death at the service and so they thought that I would be able to exonerate them from any blame. Perhaps while they were still in the throes of grief, they needed me to be there so they could confess and clear their conscience. But I was still grieving myself and I was so enraged that I could not bring myself to agree to keep whatever they told me in confidence.

I suppose that if I had been more patient, wiser, or even cleverer I would have agreed to the meeting, and we would have had those answers. But Black folks, especially Black males, are accustomed to burying their grief with anger or denial, just as surely as they bury their loved ones. Just as White Americans have become accustomed to allowing injustice and suffering to occur in the Black community, the parents of privilege in the esteemed Hyde Park Chicago community were teaching their sons and daughters that their future was more important than giving justice for Al; and easing the pain of a distraught Black family. Either directly or indirectly this is a lesson that each White generation teaches their children. They were not going to risk having the truth be known and their children's future clouded by acknowledging what really happened to a Black boy from the Southside of Chicago.

What surprised me the most at the funeral service was how many parents of Black boys told me after the service that their boys had experienced similar deaths. Their sons had been in the company of their White peers and never returned home, only to discover later that they had died in the presence of their White friends and not one of them gave the families any information regarding their son's last moments of life. I am not suggesting a conspiracy where White children are taught that Black lives don't matter, but it may be that too many signs and symbols of our society do indeed teach the general populace; young and old alike, that young Black lives are not as important as the lives of others. At the root of racism and discrimination is that Blacks are somehow different from others and not only different but are in some way evil and "devilish" and there is no sympathy for the Devil.

I believe that in Al's funeral I was seeing a precursor to the distancing and hardening of the hearts of White America toward Blacks in general and Black males in particular. The response to the city riots of the sixties, White backlash against affirmative action and the criminalization of Blacks in the Justice system would continue and gather strength in the ensuing decades. Black Lives have not mattered in our society's White majority population. I am sure that most of those White teens are still alive with families of their own. I do not know how they can live with this secret locked up in their hearts. This story and the ones before and after it are meant to emphasize that to stay out of jail and thrive, it is necessary to understand one's place in a racist society. We should not make the mistake of trusting those who do not have our best interests at heart. The criminal justice system was not meant to serve the needs of the Black, Brown, Indigenous and poor people of our nation.

Studying While Black

Much of my voluntary ministry work when I was in Boulder, CO revolved around Brothers who were dealing with the prison system. Here is a prime example of what is all too typical for Black males and law enforcement agencies. This is a redacted copy of the story of an incident that was distributed to the local community.

1—Jeffrey Neering was, Arrested, Accused, (Summer 2011) Tried and Found Guilty (November 2012) for First Degree Assault and 2nd Degree Attempted Murder after a fight with two drunken White males. One of the White males was an off-duty police officer; the other was a friend of the Supervising Police Sargent who came to the scene of the incident. The drunken police officer received a cut in the neck area and so Jeffrey was charged for two felonies. The only sober, unbiased, and credible witnesses of the incident; two White male Bouncers, stated that they saw Jeffrey being pummeled by the off-duty police officer and his friends before they (the bouncers) rescued him from the other men.

2—The Police, District Attorney and local newspaper portrayed Jeffrey as an indigent, homeless man. They did not note that he was a master's Student at Naropa University, was working two jobs and had been diagnosed with the mental health issues of bi-polar depression and substance abuse.

3—During the trial, the Police Sargent testified that he confiscated the only weapon found at the scene: a knife, which belonged to one of the White males, his friend Ollie. He testified that he gave the knife back to Ollie and re-confiscated it the next day. The knife was not thoroughly tested by the CO CSI to determine whether the knife had been cleaned before being confiscated by the police Sergeant. When the Judge asked about the whereabouts of the knife, the prosecuting District Attorney said that the knife was lost, and therefore it could not be compared to the wound or analyzed for further evidence by Jeffrey's attorney.

4—Jeffrey's mental illnesses were not mentioned during the trial. He was heavily intoxicated at the time through his attempt to self-medicate with drugs and alcohol. We are asking the community to come and support Jeffrey during the sentencing portion of his trial.

Trial and Beyond

My son Jonathon, an attorney, assured me that Jeffrey would be convicted due to his being Black in a predominantly White community. He said that we should work on having his sentence reduced after the jury found him guilty. As it was, Jeffrey faced a 32-year sentence if found guilty. The District Attorney offered a plea deal of 18 years. It was not difficult for me to believe the likelihood of Jeffrey being convicted. I had witnessed the police officer and District Attorney not blink an eye as they discussed lost evidence, testified about the incorrect handling of the evidence, and seeing a jury chosen that was not composed of Jeffrey's social or ethnic peers.

I attended every day of the trial and when I could not be there other members of the community, including some of my students who were taking a class on social justice. When I first brought this case to their attention they were not interested in the disposition of the case. It was not until a guest speaker, an older White male minister, challenged them to be concerned with their fellow classmate, did they show any interest in the case. I reasoned that if these so called progressive White liberal students didn't care about Jeffrey, then a White jury would not care either.

As my students and others observed the case, they expressed astonishment at the level of biased treatment that Jeffrey received at the hands of the police and district attorneys. They were also surprised at the ineffectiveness of his attorney as he did little to challenge the mishandling and lost evidence as grounds for appeal. Soon, other community members began to come to the trial, and they too were astonished at the way the criminal justice system treated Black males. For instance, we discovered that the other jailed prisoners kidded Jeffrey about the "White Jeffrey Neering." There was a young White man who was arrested for being in the same type of altercation that Jeffrey had but he was released after a couple of days in jail. The prisoners knew all too well, the cultural handicap that Black prisoners faced when dealing with the criminal justice system.

Other White members of the community rallied to Jeffrey's aid as they saw how unfair the proceedings were. One woman told me that she had a Black boyfriend several years ago when she learned that he had a warrant out for his arrest in another state over a dubious charge. She encouraged him to return to his home state and deal with the charge and assured him that justice would prevail. Her naivete led to her friend's returning to his home state, getting convicted and serving time in prison. She was motivated to support Jeffrey as much as she could as a way of doing penance for her previous actions.

The Arrest and Trial

Jeff's case demonstrates many of the first points expressed in this book. When he was arrested and arraigned the police had determined that he was the law breaker even though two White male witnesses at the scene testified that Jeff was the one who was being attacked by the White men. When he was arraigned, the Presiding Judge disagreed with the District Attorney's decision to charge him with two felonies. But despite this, the District Attorney convinced another judge to uphold the greater charge.

Jeffrey's attorney had not tried a felony case of this magnitude. He had little or no experience with defending a person of color who had been charged with two major felonies. Regardless, his fee of $20,000 was a cheaper price than that of more experienced attorneys in the community. His attorney only called one witness, Phil, a Naropa professor, who had no direct knowledge of the incident and like his fellow faculty members in the Religion Program, was not supportive of Jeff or other students getting the medication he needed when he was a student at the university. He even related to his classes that poor Black children were in their situation because of their bad karma. This was not the kind of witness you wanted to support a poor Black student.

During the trial, this attorney was not prepared to try such a high felony case. He had little or no experience with defending a person who had been charged with major felonies. Regardless, his fee of $20,000 was a cheaper price than that of more experienced attorneys. He did not call for a mistrial when the DA confessed that they had lost the weapon, and that the CSI Office and technicians did not do blood work or fingerprint evidence on the knife. As mentioned before, the knife itself had been confiscated by the arresting sergeant on the scene who had given it back to one of the White males involved in the incident. The CSI did not check to see if the blood evidence had been washed away by someone cleaning it before it was lost. It being "lost" helped the District Attorney's case.

His attorney only called one witness, Phil, a Naropa professor, who had no knowledge of the incident and was not supportive of Jeff getting the medication he needed when he was a student at the university. Even though Jeff wanted to take the stand in his own defense, his attorney talked him out of it, only to say later that he regretted not letting Jeffrey take the stand in his own defense.

The clincher was a phone call made by Jeff's father to him when he was in jail. He knew that the phone was monitored by the District Attorney. Even so, his father made him confess to the crime to show that he was remorseful for his part in the incident. This confession was the last thing that the District Attorney presented to the jury during the closing argument. He was found guilty as charged! Even though Jeff wanted to take the stand in his own defense, his attorney talked him out of it, only to say later that he regretted doing so.

This confession was the last thing that the District Attorney presented to the jury during the closing argument. He was found guilty as charged! Later that evening myself and another person from the school went to a local restaurant. Much to our surprise and dismay we saw the two blonde prosecuting District Attorneys celebrating with Jeff's two married male attorneys. They had told us that they were too busy with family matters to spend rehashing the case. I guess $20,000 buys a lot of pizza and beer

The Aftermath

After Jeffrey was sentenced, there was some despair, but I reminded them of what my son had predicted. We then went to work to secure as much community support as possible. We turned the Martin Luther King Jr. celebration, which before this time was barely attended, into a rally to support Jeffrey. Community members showed a film on the Civil Rights Movement. Theatre Professor, Ethelyn Friend, used her musical gifts to encourage the gathering. We organized an overnight vigil and a march which proceeded from the church to the Municipal Court where Jeffrey would be sentenced. The March was recorded and covered by the local media. The courtroom was crowded with spectators who were there to give support to Jeffrey in his time of need.

Jeffrey's mother, Forestine, had asked me to speak on Jeffrey's behalf, which I was honored to do. When Jeffrey was brought out to be sentenced the look on his face was one of astonishment. I will never forget the look of surprise and appreciation as he realized that there were many people who cared about what happened to him now and in the future. I doubt if the courtroom had ever seen this many observers for a felony case without a murder being involved.

I was somewhat amused at the number of Sheriff Deputies who were in the courtroom that day and the judge issued a stern warning that he would not tolerate any undue outbursts. I found this amusing because the crowd was composed of peace-loving members of the Boulder community. At the sentencing I and others asked the judge for mercy due to Jeffrey's incapacity at the time, and in recognition of his potential as a future scholar and valued contributor to society. The Judge gave him the lowest level of punishment possible: 12 years with 1 and 1⁄2 years served.

Jeffrey's Continuing Story

One truly compassionate student, a Buddhist Monk from Asia, began a prison ministry that was to serve Jeffrey for his first two years in prison. Jeffrey assumed a leadership position and got heavily involved in his recovery and treatment programs. Jeffrey served five years of his sentence and with time off for good behavior, he was released to a community program for reintroduction to the community. He received aid from persons like Lu W. who befriended him and made him a part of her family. Others, like Reverend Drs. Bob Balance and Stuart Lord, aided Jeffrey when he was in prison. Still others, like Buddhist Reverends, Gena Cline, came to his aid while he was in prison and during his release.

In the last year, Jeffrey announced that he was finally off parole and is in the process of completing his Master of Divinity degree. Jeff had served his time without incident, although it took me and others to constantly hold the prison authorities responsible for making sure he was receiving the proper medications he needed. All credit goes to Jeffrey and his determination not to let his past determine his future.

DRIVING WHILE BLACK

My experience of homelessness made a profound impact on my body, mind, spirits, and consciousness. Effects I would not have had if I had not been racially profiled while Driving While Black (DWB). Even though I had come up "the rough side of the mountain," as my mother would describe the hardships our family faced, there were still other more debilitating experiences that were outside the sphere of my growing up poor on the South Side of Chicago.

My homelessness was precipitated by a racial profiling incident with one of our police forces. Like so many black males I was pulled over by a policeman who claimed I was speeding. I had just moved to the area to practice as a Speech and Language Pathologist in a school system in the Midwestern United States. I had been misled by the school system official who told me I would be working with a multi-ethnic student body. Instead, the schools and students I was to serve were situated in a highly rural area in the state of Michigan. There were a few Black and Brown children and families in this community, but they were few and far between.

In order to get to these schools, I had to travel rural backroads jutting off major highways to arrive at my teaching assignments. As it was, I primarily worked with the children of poor whites whose families were struggling due to the recession of 2008. I enjoyed working with the children, but I had specialized in working with students of color since they tended to be underserved or the therapists were not trained to work effectively with this population.

To reach these schools more easily I decided to move to a place closer to the schools. When I found suitable accommodations, I was warned by the landlord that I would be travelling through a town that was notable for its penchant to treat its minority citizens badly. It was, as they put it, "red neck," country where the police had developed a reputation for stopping persons of color for the sake of intimidation and to generate revenue.

On the day I was stopped I left on a Wednesday morning, before daylight, from Elkhart, Indiana to Cass County, MI. I had just finished a Chaplain Residency Program where I worked primarily with suicidal and clinically depressed patients. It took four days to travel from the San Francisco Bay Area at Atherton, CA to Michigan. On my way to my teaching assignment, I was stopped for Driving while Black by a State Trooper in Colorado. He checked my driver's license and registration and then let me on my way. This was the tenth time I had been stopped.

When I arrived in Indiana, I was stopped by an Indiana State Trooper who informed me that my registration had expired. I was unaware of this since I had been more preoccupied with providing service as a Chaplain and planning my next move to realize that I had not renewed my license plates. I explained the situation to the officer and told him that I would take care of the registration when I was paid on Friday of next week. On this, the twelfth time I had been stopped by police, the Officer took me at my word and allowed me to go my way.

However, on the thirteenth time I was stopped, it was not due to an officer noting that my registration had expired, it was because he claimed that I was driving between 0-10 miles over the speed limit. After he checked my license and registration, he discovered that my license plate had expired. I explained to him that I just discovered the problem and that the State Trooper informed me to get it taken care of and that is what I planned to do. However, he insisted that he was going to impound my vehicle. When I explained to him that I was new to the area and was not near my home or school I was going to serve.

He said that this was not his problem and that I needed to exit the vehicle so that it could be impounded. I refused to do so, despite his statement that I would be arrested for not complying with his order. I continued to disobey his command. At that point he went to his car and called his chief. While he was talking with his chief, I was talking to mine.

I thought about being stopped, not because I was speeding, but because I was Black. I have had more complaints with my passengers because I drive so slowly and because of the previous warning, I was very careful with my speed. I was later to discover that friends of mine had also been stopped, in this part of the state because they were speeding and their registration had expired, but they were White, and did not risk officers impounding their cars in a deserted rural area. Yet, I was stopped and facing being left in a rural area because I was Black.

As I sat in the car, I felt in touch with the spirit of Rosa Parks. I had decided, like Ms. Parks, that I had taken enough racial harassment, and so when the policeman returned and ordered me out of my car again, again I refused. I asked if I were under arrest and that would be the only reason that I would leave my vehicle.

He went back to his care and informed his chief of my decision. I reiterated that I would not be leaving the vehicle unless I was placed under arrest. I explained to him my situation and that I recently travelled close to 2000 miles to help the handicapped children in his area. I also mentioned that I took this assignment even though I was recovering from a recent heart health incident. He replied that he had a bad heart as well and regardless, they were going to impound my car. He then grabbed my coat lapels with both hands to pull me out of the car. I did not resist. Once he realized that I was not going to attempt to pull away from his grasp and therefore give him cause to arrest me for the more serious crime of resisting arrest he immediately took his hands off me.

He once again asked me to leave the car. I asked if was under arrest and when he said yes, I removed myself from the car. When I asked what the charge was, he did not tell me the charge, nor did he read me my rights. When I was taken to the jail, I found out the next day that I was being charged with "attempting to obstruct" a police officer. This is a common charge that is levied against social protestors who are arrested at the scene of a protest when they refuse to obey the order by police to disperse.

I didn't realize that this arrest would result in my termination. My Black Program Director assured me that he would support me once I was released. But I was terminated due to, as the Director told me: "The White folks wanted me dismissed for causing too much trouble." Driving while Black is a personal and occupational hazard.

When I directed the Black Studies Department at UMKC I was often stopped by police as I drove from Kansas City to Jefferson to do research for a fellowship I had been awarded as a Missouri Supreme Court Historical Society Fellow. I was never given a ticket but eventually decided to take the train to prevent these numerous unwarranted stops. Missouri later changed their laws to prevent this kind of harassment.

My experience in the jail was a door that I had never entered. Like many black teens one of my biggest fears as a youth, was to be locked up in Cook County Jail in Chicago. Even back in the 50's and 60's Cook County Jail was known as a place of horrors where brutality, violence and sexual assault were the norm whether from the inmates or the guards. I felt fortunate that I had escaped experiencing the prison system and now as an older man I thought I had escaped that possibility.

My short stay in jail was revelatory. I should have been booked and released that same day but one of the county officials who interacted with prisoners told me that the officers who arrested were going to take their time in filing charges and that I would have to spend at least one night in jail to punish me and show their authority.

Another official also believed that the judge would let me off with a warning. They were wrong on both counts and was incarcerated until I could produce bail for a minor misdemeanor charge. I spent two nights in jail. One night in the holding pen with other newly arrested inmates who all had long histories of incarceration. They taught me the basic survival skills I would need in case I was held.

One of them, a Native American young man, had just been transferred from mu hometown Cook County Jail. He expressed relief that he was no longer there. I guess things have not changed much over time. The other inmates were young white males who had turned to drug activity to earn a living during the recession. They had not done well in school, and one was the son of a special education teacher and had been diagnosed with ADHD. He was a brilliant young man who taught us how to make meth, package, market and sell it.

We talked all night about the reasons for our "criminal" behavior with ranging discussions regarding the economy, the unpunished criminals on Wall Street, and the effect of their lifestyle on their families. Two of the inmates had children and they wanted to turn over a new leaf so they could be role models and providers for their children.

When they discovered that I was a university professor and minister who had chosen to be arrested they said I must be crazy. Once my identity was known one of the young white males stated that I must be laughing at them as they talked about the social and economic reasons why they were in jail. I replied that no, the quality of their arguments reminded me of some of the best discussions I had with many students during my teaching career. I promised to write about them eventually and to present their plight to a larger public. Another young white male was coming down after a drug induced high. I had decided to fast while I was in prison which was immediately spread throughout the jail.

When the young black attendant came to feed us, he gave me a short smile of admiration when I refused the meal. I found that I had to at least drink some tea because the high inmate was trying to imitate my fast and he was getting sicker. I did not want to see him suffer more than he already was and so I announced that I would take some liquid which he did as well.

They shared with me, and I shared with them. The same young man who was coming down from his high noticed a young blond girl who was in a woman's holding cell across the corridor. He stated that he thought she was in jail because she had hurt her child. Simultaneously we saw her picture flashed on the TV screen the guards kept running 24-7. She had indeed been arrested for infanticide. He began to condemn her, and I thought this was harsh seeing that he had helped destroy lives with his participation in the drug trade. I asked him if he ever heard of post- partum depression. I had noticed that she had spent most of her time kneeling over the toilet and was obviously in distress. She could see us as well I and I signaled to her that "God loves you and so do I." She teared up and thanked me before she was taken from her cell for processing.

This processing ritual is the beginning of one's dehumanization after arrest. You are ordered to take off your clothes and strip searched by the guards. A mugshot is taken, and you are given your prison garb. In my case they did not have an orange jumpsuit large enough to fit me and so I had to learn to move in such a way as to not expose my private parts.

The next day I learned what the charge was, and I was finally read my rights. And as I looked at the ticket and in the space for "race" of the person arrested was the word "unknown." This was an obvious attempt to hide the fact that they were arresting a disproportionate number of people of color. When I went before the judge, who was not present but on a TV screen, she determined that I would have to pay a bond before I could be released. I was not told about the procedure and thought that I would be asked to speak on my behalf and the guard ushered me and the others out of the room. When I asked to speak to the judge, the young White guard reacted angrily and told me that my opportunity to speak was over and that I should sit back down and be quiet. Since I did not have the money, I was placed in the general jail population. One of the younger guards asked me why I looked unhappy. I flared up and almost cursed him out. At least that was the spirit with which I replied without using offensive language.

As I was being booked, the Black officer who was doing the booking, expressed surprise at the Judge's actions, since a person of my status with no arrest record, is usually released on his own recognizance. Fortunately, there was a kind Methodist nurse there who made sure that I was given my medication. She also allowed me to call a former colleague (Merlyn) and her husband (Miklos), who were able to send the bond. I asked them to call a Pagan Unitarian Minister (Reverend Amy DeBeck) that I had recently met, who drove in the middle of the night (without telling her husband) to visit me and arrange for the bond to be paid. Because of their kindness I only had to spend two nights in jail, and I was released the next day. I will always be in debt to my white friends and white sisters who helped me in my time of need.

I was fired from my position because in the Director's words: "The White folks said I was causing too much trouble. This left me homeless since I could not pay the rent. And since I could not reach the Public Defender, my son, an attorney, stated that I could risk being convicted or leave the state. Since I could not afford to have a criminal record as I looked for further employment and I did not have the means to live in the area, I became homeless and went back to my hometown, Chicago.

The homeless situation would end after six months. My health deteriorated quickly, and I was given Social Security Disability. (SSDI) The government disability doctors told me that due to the trauma and intensity of my physical and psychological illnesses that my claim would be approved. They also said that because I had given my life in service to others, they would expedite my claim if possible. I am eternally grateful to them since I was unable to receive adequate treatment and was nearing the end of my rope.

Aftermath

I lived for eleven years with the knowledge that I had a warrant out for my arrest. This meant that if it were ever discovered that I had a warrant out for my arrest the police could have placed me under arrest. My driver's license had been revoked and I drove on an expired license for several months. I did lose two part time jobs when the employers discovered my legal status. I was also denied certification as a Speech and Language Therapist because of my record. I appealed that decision and was granted the certificate based on the merit of my rebuttal of my arrest. I realized that I could not apply for a firearm because I was officially designated as a "fugitive from justice,"

After eleven years, I was finally able to hire a lawyer and deal with this issue through a court system that was designed to move quickly if you took the plea deal and/or had the money to pay the fines. I took the plea deal, which was reduced from "attempting to obstruct a police officer," to a charge of "disturbing the peace." I paid the fine, and the lawyer bill and am now free without a warrant for my arrest.

Several friends offered to foot the lawyer bill and court fees. In the United States of America, freedom is not free. I appreciated their offers, but I did not accept their assistance. However, I told them that I intended to write about my experience, and they promised that they would buy copies of my book. Since I had been blessed monetarily by another source, I thought it more important that they support the distribution of this book which I hoped would prevent others from experiencing the plagues of jail and imprisonment in the 'home of the free and the land of the brave," Toward that end; "I cast this bread unto the waters."

PART THREE

TEACHINGS OF JESUS ON STAYING OUT OF JAIL

Jesus of Nazareth, an Afro-Asian Jewish man, was accused of being a breaker of civil laws and rebellion. False evidence was presented that depicted him as a disturber of the peace, and a potential threat to the well being of the rich and powerful. Although he was innocent of these crimes, he was arrested, charged, arraigned, judged, and sentenced. His punishment was the corporal punishment of the whip, and capital punishment by crucifixion. This is a situation that many Black and Brown Brothers of today have also experienced.

Theologians and scholars from more progressive religious backgrounds claim that he was actually a Zealot; a rebel leader who violently opposed the White European Roman Empire. More traditional conservative authors adopt the stance that he was the victim who was destined by God to be sacrificed by God as a ransom for the sins of humanity.

I argue that both groups are wrong. First of all, it is obvious that Jesus was a member of a socially oppressed community. As an Afro-Asiatic (Black and Brown) Jewish man he was on the wrong side of power. and was charged with a crime that he did not commit. The liberals are correct that he was punished in the style reserved for revolutionaries; and the conservatives are correct that he was innocent of those charges.

But they both overlook the straightforward explanation that he was victimized by the criminal justice system of his day that has been the fate of people of color in a White dominated world. Just like current times, he was a George Floyd, Trayvon Martin, Elijah McClain, Sharon Bland, Breanna Taylor, and thousands of others who have suffered lynching by a White power structure. Jesus was killed just because he was a member of a marginalized cultural group, who insisted on acting as a free person. This, in and of itself, made him a target and victim of oppressive state forces.

The traditional/conservatives of today, like the Early Hellenic Church of the first and second centuries, spiritualized and suppressed the memory of Jesus as an anti-Roman revolutionary criminal. This was to quell any possible hints of his political opposition to the White Powers. Their erasure and denial of the Radical Jesus allowed the Churches to practice their new faith in this new divine savior in peace, while accommodating and supporting the government of Rome.

Their leading theologian and apostolic messenger/spokesman, The Apostle Paul, himself a Roman citizen, hid behind his status as a Roman citizen when his freedom was threatened. The other New Testament writers wrote consistently in a manner that would prove that their Christian churches were not in opposition to the oppressive Roman Empire. They encouraged their communities to obey Roman law as if they were obeying God.

The liberal/liberation/progressive authors assume that because he was given a revolutionary's death, that he was a revolutionary. They don't understand the day to day existence of the marginalized who are constantly arrested and jailed and executed falsely as an everyday matter of their oppressive situation. Even though Jesus was certainly opposed to oppressive social structures, he did not resist them by any overt or covert political action. The Jesus of the gospels believed that God would bring a Deliverer, a Messiah, just as he had done in the times of Moses and Elijah. Some thought that he might be that Deliverer. History shows that they were wrong.

Jesus was said to have warned his followers not to engage in violent action against their White oppressors and fellow Jews who were agents of Roman rule. Not because he believed in nonviolence, but because he knew they would face destruction if they were to attack their stronger political and military oppressors. This prophetic voice would be realized a few decades after his death as Rome devastated their Jewish homeland and killed, executed, or expelled the people from their homeland.

Those who understood Jesus' message of God's love for all, bided their time until they would become the power behind the throne of the Roman Empire. Once they gained power in the 4th century CE only the indigenous North African Churches led by the Donatists and Circumcellions used whatever means necessary, including violence, to protect the poor from social oppression. Only The indigenous North African Churches of the Donatists and Circumcellions. The other Christian churches in Europe, Asia and Hellenic North African gladly cooperated with the structure and political oppression of Rome and engaged in oppressive activities of their own.

Theologians from both these groups have constructed utopias that bear little resemblance to the lives of the culturally marginalized people of color. Their middle and upper class status has distanced them from writing from the perspective of the BIPOC and the poor. What follows is my attempt to make the message of Jesus plain for those marginalized persons who are trying their best to STAY OUT OF JAIL.

If we examine the teachings of Jesus of Nazareth from the point of view of the everyday common person who was forced to live under the oppression of a foreign power, in his case, the Roman Empire, we can come to an understanding that place the gospel of Jesus of Nazareth in its proper historical setting. Taking this as the starting point for understanding the teaching of Jesus we can begin to understand that the teachings of Jesus were meant to teach his followers how to survive in an unjust and hostile world that was created by imperialism and cultural domination. This is like what Black and other persons of color face in the United States and the world. If we were to use the terms for our day and substitute the notions of categories of capitalism and race, for imperialism and culture, we would see that in his day Jesus was struggling against an early form of "White Nationalism."

The survival of Jesus' followers was intricately tied up with their ability to survive the oppressive attitudes and tactics of this greatest of "White Nationalism," that the world had yet seen. Jesus was concerned that his followers would need to be free to carry out their mission of national and personal survival against overwhelming military and economic power. Their success depended on how well they learned to stay alive and stay out of jail.

They needed to stay out of reach of the oppressive power of the social order which had occupied their land by military force, and which had instituted a system in which their own people would be responsible for keeping them in check. Jesus warned that families would be split and torn apart as a father and son, mother and sister would take different sides in relation to their allegiance to the Kingdom of God which he was bringing to earth.

Jesus not only taught his disciples: men, and women, how to survive in word, he also taught them to survive by deed. He was the perfect example of what he taught, and he lived those lessons himself. We see Jesus employ strategies and tactics of survival so that he teaches his followers by example. The lengthiest of those teachings are found in the so-called Sermon on the Mount in the Gospel of Matthew and the Sermon on the Plain in Luke. It is important then to lay out the general principles, strategies, and tactics that Jesus taught his disciples,

Nonconfrontation when faced with a more powerful enemy.

Jesus told his disciples to turn the other cheek and to not resist evil with evil. The first goal of any police encounter is to stay alive and then to stay out of prison. You are less likely to stay out of jail if the police do not have a justifiable reason to arrest you for disorderly conduct. Even the oppressor has a need to justify their unjust actions. It was possible for the White Christian nations to justify the genocide of the Native American, the Slaughter of the African Slave Trade and the Jewish Holocaust. They developed a narrative against those groups which gave those police forces who would carry out their wishes' philosophical and legally plausible reasons for their actions.

Therefore, when confronted by police, it is important to have a posture of nonviolence. Some Christian theologians have written that the non-violent posture or sayings of Jesus were the result of him believing that since the world was coming to an end that God would engage in violence against their enemies. Since that was the case, it was not necessary for his followers to take up arms against their enemies. Others have written that the message of nonviolence was only meant to be used within the Christian community and not intended to be practiced among non-Christians. Many scholars believe that

Jesus expected God to slaughter the enemies of his people especially since he knew that any attempt at violent resistance would be futile. The Roman conquerors were the greatest military force of his day and could not be successfully challenged. This was to be proven some thirty-five years after his arrest and crucifixion when the Romans destroyed Jerusalem and the Jewish Temple.

Subversive solidarity: Love for neighbor

It is my position that the case is more fundamental than that. Jesus and his followers were living in a time of violent revolution against their oppressors. The Romans were looking for any excuse to exercise their power by killing their opponents on the battlefield or by crucifixion. Jesus was not interested in having his followers befriend their Roman oppressors or their Jewish collaborators. His encounter with his fellow Jews, Zacchaeus the Tax collector, and Nicodemus the Jewish official from the Sanhedrin, the highest religious lawmaking body, revealed that Jesus only had affection for those who were willing to risk their fortune and reputation, if not their life. in the service of the Kingdom of Justice that was to come.

The response of Zacchaeus to Jesus' message was that, as a tax collector, he could no longer cheat his fellow Jewish publicans. Nicodemus, the religious official of the Sanhedrin, who were the political puppets of the Romans, could no longer "go along, to get along." Nicodemus learned that he must be "born again," and would have to live a life of service to The Kingdom that Jesus taught was being "born again."

In the well-known passage of scripture in John, which contains the most famous, but least understood verse: John 3:16, "For God so loved the world that whoever believes in Him may not perish but have eternal life." Jesus explains that being born of the Spirit is an experience that is dependent on the intention for good that a person brings to the encounter with Him.

Jesus told Nicodemus that to be born of the Spirit a person must be someone who is born in a Kingdom of love and justice. When Jesus was explaining why his opponents did not believe in his message, Jesus' reply was that:

"people loved darkness rather than light, because their deeds were evil. For every one that does evil hates the light, neither comes to the light, lest their deeds should be reproved. But they that does truth comes to the light, that their deeds may be made manifest, that they are of God". (John:3:19-21)

Like Zacchaeus, Nicodemus must have a new attitude in life in which it is more important to love the neighbor rather than enrich himself with money or power. This meant an end to exploitative, spiritual, economic, or political actions for sake the Kingdom that was to come. it was important for his disciples to practice this new style of living and remain alive and out of jail so that they could eventually be leaders of the new Kingdom. Nicodemus goes on to prove his new attitude toward life by arguing against Jesus' arrest (John 7:50-61) arrest and by helping in his burial after his crucifixion. (John 19:39-42)

Violence when necessary for survival

The biblical witness from start to finish, from Genesis to Revelations, shows God and his followers engaged in violence for a righteous cause. Nonviolence was a strategic action Jesus taught his followers so that they would not be arrested or killed by the police forces and military of their day. The Great Flood, the first violent action by God was due to the use of unjust violence by one neighbor against their neighbors. The lesson to be learned is that violence that is unjust is to be avoided at all costs because it is against the wishes of God for his creation.

It is obvious that Jesus was not against violent self-defense when it was necessary for the safety of his movement. From the scripture where he tells his disciples to take up the sword, it is evident that it was permissible to use violent means for self-defense. His ministry had a Treasure, Judas, who was in charge of feeding the poor. The fact that some of the disciples carried swords is proof that they were prepared to defend themselves from robbery and theft. John the Baptist, Jesus' mentor, and fellow prophet. taught the soldiers who came to him not to be nonviolent but that they should use violence as it was appropriate and just in their dealings with the community. (Luke 3:14)

The problem in our day is that many of our police forces and politicians do not take this teaching seriously and have erred on the side of unjust violence against those least able to protect themselves in a society that privileges European Americans and persons of wealth. The Bible is crystal clear that God often used violence as punishment for the social oppression of others. Idolatry was more than a case of worshipping idols, it had more to do with worshipping the false idols of materialism and power. The Hebrew prophets were clear about the need to treat the people, and especially the poor, with compassion. (Amos 5:24 "Let justice roll on like a river, righteousness like an ever-flowing stream.)

Put your faith in God, not the legal system. Silence is Golden

Jesus had a healthy distrust of the legal and political officials of his day whose job it was to control the populace and protect the property and interest of those in power. There is an African proverb that states that the only thing more precious than silence, is more silence. Jesus makes it plain that he intentionally disguises his true teachings because he knows that if they were understood by his enemies then they would immediately place him in jail or end his life. He tells his disciples that he talks to the crowd in parables because he knows the hearts of the men who would do him harm. When he makes the most clear and understandable statement about his mission, the officials immediately attempted to apprehend him, but Jesus miraculously escapes their clutches. His pronouncement in Luke the 4th chapter unequivocally states that he has come as a Liberator of the poor and oppressed which resulted in him having to escape the clutches of the authorities.

The Spirit of the Lord is upon me because the Lord has anointed me to preach the gospel to the poor; to heal the brokenhearted, to preach deliverance to the captives and recovering of sight to the blind, to set at liberty them that are bruised. Luke 4:18; 28-30

This clear statement, not hidden in parabolic speech, put his life in danger.

"And all they in the synagogue, when they heard these things, were filled with wrath, and rose up, and thrust him out of the city, and led him unto the brown of the hill whereon their city was built, that they might cast him down headlong. But he, passing through the midst of them, went his way," Luke 4: 28-30

Even when his mentor, John the Baptist, who is in jail for plainly speaking the truth against the political powers that be and sends his disciples to inquire of Jesus as to whether he is the Messiah,

Jesus responds with a response that answers John's question without putting himself in danger of arrest. He tells John's followers to tell John that through Jesus' ministry the people were experiencing the liberation that God promised.

"Go and show John again those things which ye do hear and see: The blind receives their sight, and the lame walk, the lepers are cleansed, and the deaf hear, the dead are raised up, and the poor have the gospel preached to them. And blessed is the one who is not offended by me." (Matthew 11:4-6)

Jesus is not a politician.

He has no political theology, except the theology of God's love for the poor. He did not have a message that could be pigeonholed in such a way that he could be easily targeted for arrest. His theology of love meant that he desires for his followers to have an abundant life that is possible only if they were willing to sacrifice their own egos for the sake of the coming Kingdom.

But he is not naïve when speaking about the way his followers should live their lives. His parable about the widow woman who constantly nags the unrighteous judge until he grants her justice is only all too familiar for those who live under social oppression.

And he (Jesus) spake a parable unto them to this end, that men ought always to pray, and not to faint; Saying, There was in a city a judge, which feared not God, neither regarded man: And there was a widow in that city; and she came unto him, saying, Avenge me of mine adversary. And he would not for a while: but afterward he said within himself, Though I fear not God, nor regard man; Yet because this widow troubleth me, I will avenge her, lest by her continual coming she weary me.

(Luke 18:1-5)

In another parable he tells his followers to "count the cost' when faced with an enemy of superior force. He does not tell them to be nonviolent in every situation. Instead, they must be sure that their actions have the best chance for success. (Luke 14:25-33)

A Lack of money is the root of evil for most.

There is a biblical teaching that the "love of money is the root of all evil. (1Timothy 6:1) What goes unsaid is obvious; the poor lack because the rich have more than they need and will not share with the needy. Jesus was clear that the rich who neglected the poor could expect to suffer when they died. (Luke 16:19-31) He is also clear in that same chapter that those who wish God's favor cannot love God and the pleasures of this world. A person's loyalty is known to what they give their heart. If wealth becomes the object of worship, the will of God cannot be accomplished.

Jesus' enemies tried to trap him into saying something treasonous against the government when they asked him whether they should have to pay taxes to the government. His answer of: "Give to Caesar the things of Caesar and give to God, the things that are of God," (Mark 12:17) was his way of saying that their priority should be how they could help the poor and not use unfair taxation as a reason for political and civil rebellion.

Jesus does not allow his enemies to decide where and when he will die for his cause. He continually avoids any confrontations that will lead to his enemies placing him under arrest. His response to his enemies who wish him to make treasonous statements about Rome are an example of his tactics. We can learn much from Jesus' attitudes and actions regarding the legal system of his day. He is an expert at subverting its power by a carefully thought-out program of strategic compliance with police forces, obeying civil laws, silence regarding seditious political statements and avoidance of religious enemies.

When you go with your adversary to the magistrate (judge) as you are in the way, give diligence that you may be delivered from him; lest they take you to the judge, and the judge deliver you to the police and the police throw you into prison. (Luke 12:58)

A practical bit of advice is do not involve oneself in the court system if it can at all be avoided. This is especially true for Black men who are seeking custody of their children. I have worked with too many Black men who have attempted to work within the court system to be at all encouraged by their interaction with a system that is all too often more concerned with dissolving the family by removing the father from the home or life of the child, even when all evidence would suggest the opposite.

There is a tendency to spiritualize the teachings and parables of Jesus. In a country where the powerful are trying to hide the anti-racist and anti-materialism positions that exist within the scriptures it becomes too easy to make a plain parable "walk on all fours." Those who heard Jesus were victims of social oppression and they understood how to interpret the parables of Jesus as examples of how systemic injustice worked in their own lives.

PART FOUR

SOCIAL THEORY AND JAILING

Rapetalism

The social theory that I use to analyze the contemporary and historical times of the United States is "Rapetalism." Rapetalism is defined as the interaction between the systemic injustices of racism, sexism, and capitalism. It is a matrix that can be applied to particular social situations. It has governed the way Europeans and European Americans, or Whites, as they call themselves, have proceeded to exploit the darker, poorer, and differently gendered persons of the world. If I were to draw a Venn diagram it would look like this:

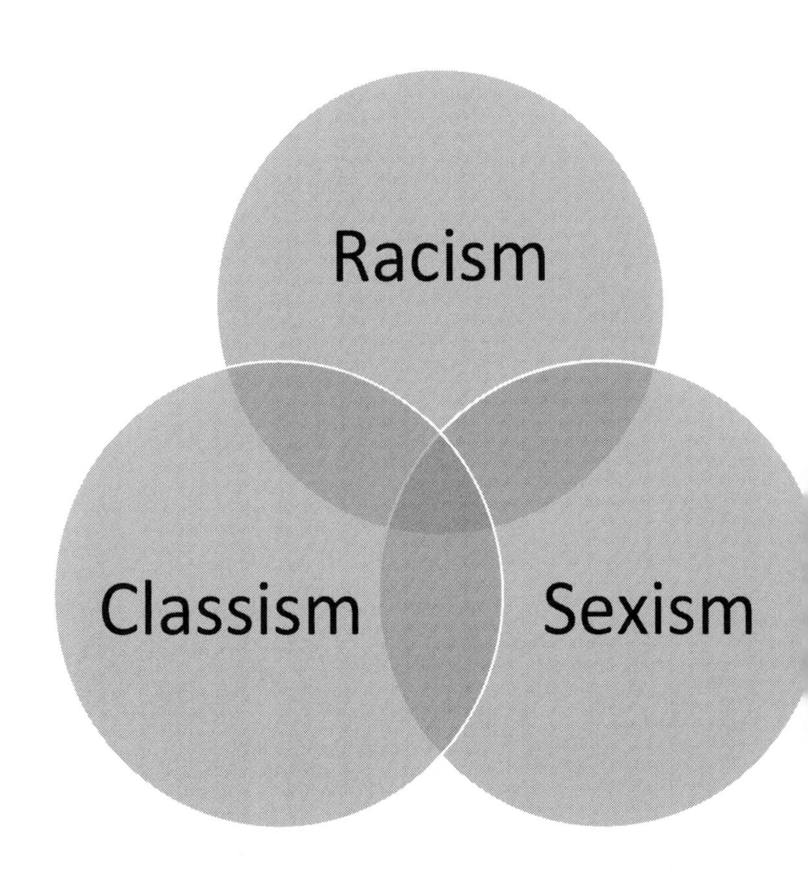
Racism
Classism
Sexism

The underlying theory for this book came out of an intense conversation with my homies as we sat in the C Shop at the University of Chicago. We were aspiring Doctoral students in theology, philosophy, sociology, business, law, economics, and social work, to name a few. We had formed The Black Graduate Forum which was meant to foster a sense of community for Black graduate students.

In forming this student group, we had been warned by university officials that we would have their support as long as we didn't become "political." The University of Chicago is known for its lack of empathy for student sponsored political demonstrations. During the 1960's they were less tolerant of students who had missed classes in protest of the Vietnam War and many of those students found themselves under suspension or the recipients of other punishments. Of course, we ignored that "advice" and immediately sponsored talks by social scientists, John and Jean Comaroff, and William Julius Wilson (now at Harvard) concerning some of the important political issues facing the Black Diaspora communities. We were also full participants in the movement to have the university divest from South African companies as a part of the anti-apartheid movement.

As we engaged in one of our heated discussions about the causes for the social and psychological oppression of Black people the discussion reached a fevered pitch. I was suddenly moved to stand up and say, "*It's Rapetalism*!" My colleagues looked at me with shock and curiosity. I began to explain that it meant that the suffering of Blacks was a combination of racial, sexual, and economic oppression, and that an analysis that only looks at the situation of Blacks through a single lens was shortsighted to say the least. This was before the use of the term "intersectionality" by critical race theorists. Also, scholars from middle and upper middle class backgrounds were often blinded to some of the deeper ways in which Rapetalistic oppression of Black males.

They may have applied a triple analysis to the plight of Black women of color, but Black men were often left out of this analysis. Our more progressive scholars and society may express mild to strong empathy for the oppression of women, queer, and the poor, but Black men, if they were seen as victims of oppression, it was seen as due to their race and economic status, but not because of their gender. Yet, this book will argue that they suffer extreme forms of oppression exactly because they are males. Black males to be more precise. They too suffer from GENDERED Oppression just as do their sisters of color. The mass incarceration of Black males. The frequent police killings of

Black males. The lower economic and health status of Black males has received little social acknowledgement or specific programs due to the erasure of a gendered analysis as a vital means of understanding the nature of Black Male gendered oppression.

The effects of Rapetalistic oppression are many and varied. Its effects are readily seen when examining issues of social justice in the Black community. For instance, Americans are intrigued when these three social forces are present in any one situation. The trial of O.J. Simpson was a prime example when issues of race, gender and class were on the front stage of American consciousness. The fact that Simpson, a wealthy Black man, was accused of murdering a White woman and her male friend from a lower income status, put all three areas of Rapetalism in play. The previous examples I gave of the ten factors in jailing are easily seen. In this case, Simpson was able to gain his freedom because he was wealthy and could afford the best legal representation possible, and his prime attorney, Johnny Cochran, a Black man, was able to take advantage of the long-standing conflict between the Los Angeles Police Department and the jurors, who were primarily Black.

Simpson being declared innocent was the result of the hundreds of years of distrust between the Black community and White government policing authorities. Also, the more recent and continuing flaunting of Black persons' rights by those authorities left a bad taste in the mouths of the jurors. Therefore. when Simpson's attorneys brought up the possibility of the police planting evidence, or the history of racial bias by one of the lead detectives on the case, Mark Furman, that was enough to convince the jury that the case against O.J. did not meet the standard of "beyond a reasonable doubt."

I have spoken to many Black persons of all social statuses, rich and poor, male, and female, young and old, and most of them agreed that in all likelihood Simpson did commit the murders or at least was heavily involved in some way. But, almost to a person, they believed due to their own personal experiences, that the police had probably tampered with the evidence and there was a sense of satisfaction, that at least one Black man, regardless of his lack of a Black identity, had not been convicted of a crime.

This Rapetalistic American consciousness has extended to many high-profile cases. The trials of the "Mikes;" Michael Jackson and Mike Tyson, are examples of the extraordinary interest that Americans have when in the presence of these three factors. This is especially true for Black males since Black men have long been stereotyped as violent sexual threats; and are more likely to be engaged with the criminal justice system. This Rapetalistic consciousness also exists at the everyday level of the Black male encounter with police. There is a historically based fear of the Black men that White police officers have internalized due to their exposure to symbolic images and narrative tales of Black depravity that have been a part and parcel of the American media. From the "Black rapist freedman" in Cecil DeMille's milestone American movie; to the Black exploitation movies of the 70's and seen in Gangsta Rap songs and videos of the 80's on in which Black males are pictured as oversexed, violent criminals, this image of the dangerous Black man who deserves to be incarcerated continues to structure the feelings of the White populace.

Even the election of a Black President has not been enough to combat this overwhelming image of the Black male. The police killings of Black men like; Michael Brown, Eric Garner, Oscar Grant, Trayvon Martin, Philando Castille, Elijah McClain and hundreds of others, including several Black women like Breanna Taylor and Sandra Bland, bear witness to the depth of the fear and loathing that centuries of American Rapetalistic narratives have created in White Americans toward their Black citizens.

The release of O.J. Simpson and the conviction of Derrick Chauvin, for the George Floyd murder both speak to the importance of the last four (7-10) factors that I wrote about earlier. In each case the presence of excellent attorneys, adequate monetary resources, community pressure and social media, made the difference in the outcome of these cases. These factors are often in dialectical relationship to each other. Adequate legal representation is often linked to adequate economic resources (Cash is King). Community pressure and social media often go hand in hand in today's world of the internet. Community pressure can be generated through the internet and the internet can generate community pressure. The most prominent attorneys are often attracted to take cases that have a high community profile.

The problem with much of public concern with the jailing of poor Black and Brown persons is that they do not develop adequate monetary resources for persons who do not have the high profile of the persons above. Instead of marching for marching's sake, it is more important to develop community resources that can be of direct aid to persons who are the most in danger of facing the criminal justice system without adequate representation and support. Some of these groups; both the old time Civil Rights organizations and the new groups led by the Black Lives Matter advocates have raised millions of dollars that are primarily spent on the organization itself instead of funding adequate financial assistance for accused persons. Often, they do not have achievable goals that can result in more justice for poor persons of color.

At one point, groups like the NAACP and ACLU had provided legal assistance that represented persons facing imprisonment. But this activity was geared toward some higher goal of changing discrimination laws. As it stands now, persons of color and the poor, have few resources for the achievement of a just outcome. New and fresh approaches are needed to develop more grassroots programs that will have an immediate impact.

Some of these programs could involve:

-Mental Health Assistance for at risk and incarcerated youth and adults

-Legal Defense Fund for Poor Persons of Color.

-Bail funds or campaigns to eliminate bail for persons who cannot afford it.

-Community education for police interaction

-Job assistance for the formerly incarcerated.

-Educational and vocational internships for at risk youth.

-Anti-Rapetalistic education for Criminal Justice Professionals and Students

-Community reporting on the causes of imprisonment at the local level.

It is possible to examine the examples I gave of how myself and others were treated by the criminal justice system. The factor of race was pervasive throughout these examples. The role of gender/sexual oppression was also present. Unfortunately, it is usually not recognized that Black males are not the victims of oppression because of their race, but also because of the way their gender role has been constructed to increase the fear of them simply because they are male and Black. The presence of economic oppression is also present in these instances since most of the Black community is sorely lacking in wealth due to hundreds of years of slavery and discrimination which deprived the Black community of recompense for their labor.

It is difficult to deal effectively with a criminal justice system that is structured in a society that lives out this Rapetalistic matrix of racial, sexual, and economic oppression. When a Black person is confronted due to their racial status, there remains the presence of gender and/or economic factors that must be overcome for justice to occur. This triple matrix of exploitation has normally been applied to the status of Black women due to their brutal sexual exploitation during slavery. However, what historians and social scientists have rarely acknowledged, is that Black males were often forced to engage in sexual relationships by slaveowners who wanted to increase their investment in human capital. The objectification of the Black male continued through the Jim Crow Era with lynching and the mass incarceration of Black males after the Civil Rights Movement.

The vestiges of this Rapetalistic system are still intact as Black men continue to disproportionately suffer social ills just because they are Black and male. Black men are the largest homeless population, the largest incarcerated social group, and are the less likely of all men in the United States to be able to develop stable sexual and familial relationships due to a lack of educational and economic resources and opportunities.

There is much more that can be said about the ways in which it is important to "stay out of jail." My son Jonathan, the attorney, emphasizes that if you are going to be arrested, make sure that it happens before Thursday so that you don't get caught up in a system in which the police can hold you for two days before you can be arraigned by a judge. Otherwise, you are likely to spend a long weekend in jail. He said this partly in jest because a person has little control over what day they are going to be arrested. Yet, the important point is that one must be cautious when interacting with police forces. Remember the ten points I wrote about and do your best to **STAY OUT OF JAIL**

Your Brother,

Dr. Don, The Homeless Professor

Why I Am The Homeless Professor

Love is ego-less action for the other.
I am homeless because I was racially profiled by police, jailed for three days, lost my job because of it, went back to Chicago where I was homeless in the Winter Hell where Jesus changed my name.
I am homeless because my God is homeless so that S/He can be present with you and me.
I am homeless like the millions in jails and those who lost their homes and lies due to the Rapetalistic (Racial, Sexual and Economic Oppression) cultures in which we dwell.
I am homeless because I was stolen from my African home and brought to America to build the wealthiest homeland in the world for those who killed, raped, tortured, and discriminated against my people.
I am homeless like my Father Abraham who was looking for a home not made with human hands whose builder and maker was God.
I am homeless like my Ancestor Moses who chose to leave his home of gold in order to be with his people out in the cold.
I am homeless like John the Baptist living in the desert near the Dead Sea where he was beheaded in his quest to be free.

I am Homeless like my Jesus who had nowhere to lay his head before he was laid in an empty tomb.
I am homeless like the Buddha whose home was underneath a Banyan tree where he experienced serenity and peace.
I am homeless like The Prophet Muhammad who was forced to flee from Mecca to Medina at the point of a sword.
I am homeless because a stable nor a ghetto, a refugee camp, or detention center is a home.
I am homeless because I have made Heaven my Home and my True home is in the Kingdom of heaven which is within.
I told Jesus it would be alright if he changed my name. Jesus changed my name to

Dr. Don, PhD

Donald Henry Matthews-Bio

Donald H. Matthews is retired and now lives in University Place, Washington. He received his Ph.D. from The Divinity School at The University of Chicago (Religion and the Human Sciences: (The Sociology and Psychology of Religion), Master of Divinity, The Pacific School of Religion, Berkeley, CA, B.S, M.A, Communication Disorders, Northwestern University, Evanston, Il. He is a licensed Baptist and ordained Methodist minister, Chaplain, ACPE.

His first book, "Honoring the Ancestors: An African Cultural Interpretation of Black Religion and Literature," was published by Oxford University Press. He has written numerous books, articles, and papers, and has taught at several universities and seminaries, including Central Michigan University (Religion and Philosophy Dept.), Temple University (Religious Studies Dept), Chicago Theological Seminary, (Tenured in Religion and Society),The University of California at Santa Cruz, (Visiting Professor American Studies}, Colgate-Rochester-Crozier Divinity School, Rochester, NY (History and Black Church Studies), and St. Louis University (Tenure in the Department of Sociology). He was The Director of the Black Studies Program at The University of Missouri Kansas City and

Coordinator of The Master of Divinity Program at Naropa University. He currently resides in the Seattle, Washington area in Tacoma/University Place where he has served as an Adjunct Professor at The University of Puget Sound in the Black Studies Department, Tacoma Community College and Advisor and Lecturer at MICAH: the Minnesota Institute of Contemplation and Healing.